The Early French Explorers of North America

EXPLORATION AND DISCOVERY

EXPLORATION AND DISCOVERY

The Early French Explorers of North America

How Giovanni Verrazano, Jacques Cartier,
Samuel de Champlain, Étienne Brûlé, and
others explored the wilderness
and established French settlements

Daniel E. Harmon

Mason Crest Publishers
Philadelphia

Produced by OTTN Publishing, Stockton, N.J.

Mason Crest Publishers
370 Reed Road
Broomall PA 19008
www.masoncrest.com

3 5 7 9 8 6 4 2

Library of Congress Cataloging-in-Publication Data

Harmon, Daniel E.
  The early French explorers of North America / Daniel E. Harmon.
      p. cm. — (Exploration and discovery)
Summary: Discusses the adventures of the first French explorers of
North America, including Giovanni da Varrazano, Jacques Cartier, Etien
Brule, Samuel de Champlain, and Jean Nicolet.
  Includes bibliographical references and index.
  ISBN 1-59084-044-5
1. America—Discovery and exploration—French—Juvenile literature.
2. North America—Discovery and exploration—French—Juvenile
literature. 3. Canada—History—To 1763 (New France)—Juvenile
literature. 4. Explorers—America—History—Juvenile literature.
5. Explorers—France—History—Juvenile literature.
[1. North America—Discovery and exploration—French. 2. Explorers.]
I. Title. II. Exploration and discovery (Philadelphia, Pa.)
E131 .H37 2003
970.01'8—dc21
                                                        2002008527

EXPLORATION AND DISCOVERY

Contents

A bridge spans the mighty St. Lawrence River, which flows between present-day Canada and the United States. During the 16th and 17th centuries, French adventurers explored the St. Lawrence River, and much of North America, hoping to find a way to the rich lands of Asia.

A Foothold in the New World

LAP-SWISH…Lap-swish…Lap-swish…Lap-swish….

With each deep pull of the broad paddles, the birchbark canoe surged a few more yards over the surface of the St. Lawrence River. The sky was gray; the cloud cover high. There would be no snow today—but the cold sting of the lake breeze on their swarthy, bearded cheeks told the Frenchmen winter was on its way. Perhaps tomorrow, or the next day, would come the first stinging flurries. By then, they hoped to be at the frontier town. There, a crackling fire and hot bread would chase the weariness from their bones. And they had stories to tell!

The year was 1620. The French traders in their red

stocking caps were returning from a season of hunting and trapping in the wilderness around the lake country. The Indians knew the forests well, but few white men visited the region.

These were men of the second generation in New France—the settlers determined to make their livings, if not their fortunes, here. The first explorers who had come to North America the previous century had little intention of staying. This continent blocked the way to a far more alluring place: the Orient, the land we today know as Asia.

The quest for the Orient was what had brought the French here to begin with. Centuries before, an overland trader named Marco Polo had traveled from Italy to China and brought back valuable spices and silks to his European homeland. After it became clear, in the late 1400s and early 1500s, that the earth was round, the governments and bankers of Europe turned their attention to the Atlantic Ocean. They were frustrated by the land route between western Europe and Asia because it was extremely long, difficult, and dangerous. It would take overland expeditions years to complete a round trip—if they got back at all. Perhaps the best way to the fabled treasures of the Orient was by sailing all the way around the world.

Adventurous sea captains and army commanders and governors appointed by their kings set forth from the coasts of Portugal, Spain, France, and England. The first of them, men like Christopher Columbus, believed they had reached the Orient when they stumbled ashore in the surf of the West Indies Islands and the eastern coast of North America. Soon, however, they realized this was not the place described by Marco Polo—this was a new land altogether. It was fascinating in its own way, but it was not what they sought. They must find a way around it or through it and proceed by ship to China.

During 1519–1522, the crew of Ferdinand Magellan, sailing for Spain, managed to sail all the way around the world (Magellan himself was killed by natives in the Pacific Ocean). The route they took was hardly appealing to other *mariners*. Magellan had sailed south along the coast of South America and through the stormy Strait of Magellan. There had to be a more direct, safer way.

In France, King Francis I sent a major *expedition* across the Atlantic in 1524. Its leader was not a Frenchman, but an Italian. Giovanni da Verrazano was a *navigator* who already had much experience sailing the Mediterranean and the eastern Atlantic. King Francis hired him to make the dangerous voyage westward on behalf of France.

Some bold French seafarers were already familiar with lands far north of where Columbus had landed. By 1504, French saltwater fishermen were braving the North

King Francis I of France believed his country should match the accomplishments of Spain, Portugal, and England, all of which had sent exploring parties to the New World. King Francis sponsored the voyages of Giovanni da Verrazano, as well as trips by Jacques Cartier, one of the greatest French explorers of the 16th century.

Atlantic to harvest the fish-rich waters of the Grand Banks, off the coast of Newfoundland. French fisheries could send crews twice a year: cod fishermen to the Grand Banks in early spring, and whalers across the Arctic fringes in summer. Some of these crews ventured along the shorelines of Newfoundland and Nova Scotia.

In 1507, one of the French fishing vessels unloaded a cargo much more exciting than the tons of codfish by which the seamen earned their living: seven Indians from Newfoundland. The sailors called them "savages"—the name future French explorers would commonly apply to Native Americans.

Supported by King Francis and some Italian bankers, Verrazano sailed in January 1524 aboard *La Dauphine*, a ship he had borrowed from the French navy. *La Dauphine* was large for its day, weighing 100 tons and manned by a crew of 50 sailors.

Giovanni da Verrazano was born in 1485 to a noble family. Historians believe he may have accompanied at least one fishing expedition to Newfoundland while in his 20s.

After surviving a monstrous winter storm, Verrazano came safely to the American coast at what is present-day Cape Fear, North Carolina. He sailed southward for several days. Then, fearing he would run into Spanish warships that prowled the warmer waters in that direction, he turned northward.

For 1,000 miles, Verrazano explored the North American coastline. Occasionally, he sent men ashore for food and water. They were impressed by the natives— Verrazano described some of them as "sharp-witted, nimble, and great runners." In one place, the sailors took a Native American child from its mother as a "souvenir" of their journey. Most of the natives they met treated these strange, bearded men from the sea with kindness and curiosity. One exception was the Abnaki tribe on the coast of present-day Maine. Although they eventually agreed to trade with the

Frenchmen, they frightened Verrazano's men with their wild appearance, war cries, and attacks with bows and arrows. Because of them, Verrazano called their land *Terra Onde di Mala Gente*: "Land of Bad People."

Verrazano went as far north as Newfoundland. Although he saw many inlets and passages that extended beyond the western horizon, he could not identify a clear route around or through this new land. He was forced to return to Europe with a fairly unsatisfactory report. The one thing Verrazano had proved, however, was that these lands across the sea were not part of Asia.

For several years, Verrazano sought backing for another voyage. At last, he raised anchor in the French port of Dieppe in the spring of 1527. This time, he crossed the Atlantic far to the south. After talking his way out of a **mutiny** by his crew, he reached the coast of Brazil and returned to Europe with a cargo of rare wood.

In 1528, Verrazano set sail for the west again. We do not know whether he reached America this time, for he did not return. Historians believe he may have been murdered by cannibals on the island of Guadeloupe in the Caribbean Sea.

Verrazano had failed to reach the Orient and, in fact, had lost his life trying. Critics have determined that he contributed little to Europeans' knowledge of the New World.

Like Christopher Columbus, Giovanni da Verrazano was an Italian sailor who made his discoveries for the ruler of a foreign country, in this case France. Verrazano explored the Atlantic coast of North America for more than a thousand miles, from the present-day state of South Carolina to New York.

A cautious explorer, he usually anchored far offshore, safe from Indian arrows. He apparently missed finding the great Chesapeake and Delaware bays on his first voyage. He also failed to investigate the mouth of the Hudson River at what would become one of the world's largest and most important ports, New York.

But Verrazano had taken important first steps in exploring North America. Other French explorers—and settlers—soon would follow.

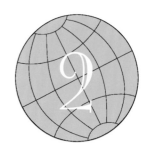

The Voyages of Jacques Cartier

KING FRANCIS LET the matters of finding the Orient and exploring New France rest for a few years. He had more important problems to worry about at home. But in the 1530s, the king decided to try again. If there was an easy way to reach the Orient with its spices and gems—and perhaps great quantities of gold and silver—then France must find it first. The European country that discovered the sea route, King Francis knew, could control trade with the East.

At the same time, a rivalry was developing between the European powers over territory in the Americas. If nothing else, Francis knew he must establish French *colonies* in New France to keep up with the other countries. So the king

15

commissioned an experienced seafarer named Jacques Cartier to sail west to North America.

Born in 1491, Cartier was from a well-to-do family. He made seafaring his career, and may at one time have been a kind of sea captain known as a **corsair**. This was a kind of pirate, except that he operated with the support of his country's king. Corsairs roamed the Atlantic, Mediterranean, and Caribbean. They attacked ships that flew enemy flags, stealing their valuables and sometimes taking the foreign ships for their own use.

Cartier sailed from France in April 1534, commanding 60 men in two frail wooden ships. It was a little early in the year to be traveling the North Atlantic, for the fringes of the Arctic icepack were melting with the spring warmth and icebergs were drifting southward. Cartier and his men saw lots of ice, but they managed to dodge the dangers. They reached Newfoundland in only three weeks—a remarkably quick **transatlantic** passage in those days.

Cartier did not find a route through New France that would lead to China. He investigated the great Gulf of St. Lawrence, however, and met and traded with some of the coastal Indian tribes. He claimed for France the shoreline and islands he found and raised a wooden cross on the shore of the Bay of Gaspé, much to the dismay of the local Indians. The natives weren't sure what the visitors were

Cartier lived in St. Malo, a French port famous for its tough and successful fishermen. At this time, French fishermen had begun crossing the Atlantic and casting their nets off the coast of modern-day Canada. Foremost among these bold, long-range laborers were the fishermen of St. Malo. Cartier probably grew up captivated by exciting tales of violent storms, sea monsters, and daring adventures on the open ocean.

doing, but they sensed Cartier was staking a claim to their land. Through gestures and broken language, the French told the Indians that they merely needed the cross as a landmark for future voyages. If the natives weren't exactly convinced by what the French said, they were somewhat satisfied by the *trinkets* Cartier's men gave them.

Exploring its inlets and islands, Cartier was impressed by much of what he saw. Some areas were bleak, with poor soil. Others were green and beautiful, although wild. There, Cartier imagined, French farmers might do very well. Fishermen could thrive on the bountiful coastal waters.

Just as important were the native people he met. Some of them, at least, were friendly. They wore animal furs. How

The Dangerous Atlantic Crossing

Crossing the Atlantic was a long and dangerous undertaking in the years of the early explorers. Christopher Columbus had been at sea for 33 days when he came to the island of San Salvador in the Bahamas in 1492. For the next two centuries, transatlantic voyages would take from several weeks to several months, depending on the weather, the captain's wisdom, and the crew's experience and skill. It took Jacques Cartier three weeks to make his first voyage from France to Newfoundland in 1534.

The crossing was not for the timid. Everyone who boarded a tiny, crowded wooden ship bound over the sea knew he or she might never arrive. Even into the 20th century, many an oceangoing vessel vanished into the deep ocean without a trace.

Besides violent storms, sailors often were stricken with diseases such as scurvy, caused largely by their unbalanced diets and the poor sanitary conditions aboard ship. If they remained at sea too long, they faced threats of starvation and food poisoning. On more than one occasion, ship crews became so discontent or frightened that they mutinied, killing the captain or locking him in chains.

Thousands of bold sailors, settlers, hunters, and fishermen were willing to take the risk, however. Samuel de Champlain, a famous leader of New France in the early 1600s, crossed the Atlantic almost two dozen times!

the French visitors' eyes must have widened as they gazed on the thick, hairy hides, highly prized by fashionable Europeans.

He did not realize it, but Cartier was looking at the real source of wealth in New France. It was a kind of treasure the kings of Europe had not expected and did not fully appreciate. Fur skins were popular and of some value, certainly, but where was the gleaming gold? Yet, the fur trade would be the foundation for three centuries of French exploration and settlement in Canada and the United States.

For the moment, Cartier, like his backers in France, was more interested in gold. He was intrigued by Indians' stories of a great kingdom called Saguenay in the forests to the west. Gold, copper, precious jewels, and other riches could be found there, the French were told.

Cartier had to return to France at the end of summer. His ships already were hampered by contrary winds, and he knew the autumn storm season would make further exploration more dangerous.

In 1535 Cartier returned with three ships and more than 100 men. He wanted to find Saguenay. This time, he entered the mouth of the mighty St. Lawrence River. For the first time, the French were poised to explore the interior of what is today known as Quebec province.

Along the banks of the broad waterway lived the

Jacques Cartier claims the Gaspé peninsula for France in 1534. Unlike in this engraving, in which the natives are sitting calmly by as Cartier's men erect a cross on the peninsula, the Indians of the region were angry when they saw the explorer staking a claim to their territory.

Iroquois people. Notable Indian villages stood on the sites of present-day Quebec, near the point where the St. Lawrence narrows, and Montreal, 125 miles farther inland. It was Cartier who gave Montreal its name. When he arrived, it was an Indian town called Hochelaga. Cartier called a nearby mountain Mont Royal, or "Royal Mountain."

The French city of Montreal was not actually founded until a century after Cartier's explorations. By 1642, it was a major fur-trading center of New France.

Cartier explored as far as the Lachine Rapids, an impassable section of the St. Lawrence near Hochelaga. Autumn had arrived, and

Cartier decided to settle in for the winter rather than risk a return across the hurricane-blown Atlantic. His men built a crude fortress at a place called Stadacona, near present-day Quebec, while Cartier explored more of the region.

Winter was unexpectedly harsh. The French ships were stuck in the iced-over river. Perhaps in part because the French mistreated them, the Indians became less friendly and even aggressive. Without their help, it was difficult for Cartier's party to obtain food. Hungry and cold, almost the

New France

The French land in North America claimed by Verrazano, Cartier, and other explorers eventually became known as New France. In the years that followed, French settlers prospered in three regions of North America: what today is the lower part of the provinces of Quebec and Ontario; Acadia (the modern maritime provinces of Nova Scotia, New Brunswick, and Prince Edward Island); and, far to the south, Louisiana on the Gulf of Mexico.

The Louisiana settlement was not established until nearly a century after the French Canadian settlements, and most historians generally are referring to the Canadian part of these holdings when they speak of New France. This was where three-fourths of the early French adventurers and missionaries explored and set down roots.

Cartier and members of his crew, cheered by Native Americans, paddle up the St. Lawrence River in small boats in this painting. Cartier explored the river during his 1535 voyage.

entire French crew fell ill with *scurvy*. Eventually, however, the Indians taught them how to treat the disease using a certain type of tree bark.

When the French returned to France in May of 1536, they took Donnaconna, the local chief, and a few other natives with them by force. Cartier planned to offer the Indians as gifts to his king. He also wanted Donnaconna to tell the king about Saguenay, the legendary Indian kingdom of fabulous riches (which, as it turned out, did not exist). Kidnapping the Indians had tragic results. All but one of them would die quickly in France. This was because their bodies were exposed to European infectious diseases that they had no resistance against.

For the next several years, the French government had serious problems at home. France frequently was at war with Spain or England, and the king had no money to spend on expeditions to the New World. Cartier did not return to North America until 1541.

A French nobleman known by the title Sieur de Roberval (his real name was Jean-François de La Rocque) wanted to start a permanent colony in New France. Since Roberval was willing to pay the expenses himself, the government had no objections. Roberval was given the title **viceroy**, or governor, of New France.

Roberval knew he needed a veteran sea captain familiar with the strange region across the ocean and with the people who lived there. He recruited Cartier, who was eager to return. Cartier was given an impressive title: captain-general of Roberval's fleet of ships. Roberval, however, had overall authority over the expedition.

Roberval was not ready to leave France at the appointed time, so Cartier set out with several of the ships on May 23, 1541. They arrived at Stadacona three months later. There, they set about preparing winter quarters—and another unpleasant winter it was. This time, the French knew how to prevent the dreaded scurvy, but the Indians were more hostile than before. They began attacking wood-cutters from the French fort. By winter's end, natives had killed more than 30 of Cartier's settlers.

By June of 1542, Cartier had decided it was unsafe to remain at Stadacona. He loaded up his ships and headed for France. As Cartier was sailing toward the Atlantic through the Gulf of St. Lawrence, he saw French ships heading his way. They belonged to Roberval, who had finally arrived— almost a year late—to lead his colony. Roberval ordered Cartier to turn around and go with Roberval's ships to Stadacona, but Cartier apparently had had enough of New France. The record of what happened is not clear, but some historians believe Cartier's ships quietly slipped away under the cover of darkness. Roberval would have to carry out his plans without Cartier's help.

Roberval found conditions around Stadacona no less miserable than Cartier had. He also found that the people he had brought with him to colonize New France were not agreeable settlers to work with. Many of them enjoyed quar-reling much more than working. Roberval had to punish them severely—one was even executed. The French were in a dark mood as winter came on.

This winter was even colder than the year before. Roberval's settlers shivered constantly, fell ill with scurvy (about 50 died), and fearfully watched their supplies of food dwindle away. The following spring, Roberval briefly set out by canoe to try to find the elusive kingdom of Saguenay. Some of his men drowned when their vessel overturned in river rapids. Roberval sailed home to France in defeat.

For the next half century, the French government made little effort to support its settlers in the New World. The home country was torn by a religious war between Catholics and Protestants, who were called Huguenots. Only fishermen continued to cross the ocean's expanse and make their living from Newfoundland's waters.

Historians are not sure whether Jacques Cartier made any notable voyages after 1542. Already, however, he had made his mark in history as the "founder of New France." He died of a plague 15 years later in St. Malo.

Grasset St Sauveur inv. direx   J. Laroque Sculp

Sauvage Iroquois

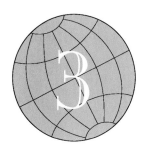

The People of North America

WHO WERE THE Native Americans the French encountered when they came to the New World? What did they look like? What did they eat? Did they live the lives of wandering nomads, sleeping on the ground in the forest?

Many different tribes lived in what are now Canada and the United States. They grew squash, corn, and other crops. They hunted the woods and fished the rivers and streams; those who lived along the coasts killed seals and other saltwater game. Most lived in villages with primitive huts or in longhouses that could shelter many families.

French woodsmen soon learned that the Native Americans from different territories gathered at certain

A reconstruction of Fort Michilimackinac, one of the most famous French trading posts of the 17th century. This wilderness outpost was a place where French woodsmen could bring their furs and exchange them for supplies; the French also traded with the Native Americans here.

wilderness *rendezvous* areas. There, they traded corn, tobacco, wild rice, flint, animal hides, and other items. The best-known rendezvous during the years of French exploration and settlement was Michilimackinac. A primitive port along the waters between lakes Michigan and Huron, it attracted buffalo-hunting peoples from the west and farmers and fishermen from the east.

During the 1600s Michilimackinac was an important frontier destination for French traders, trappers, and explorers. The Europeans brought their metal tools and colorful clothes to the *pow-wows*. They also introduced the tribes to muskets and gunpowder. These new weapons gave the Indians great advantages in hunting. All too soon, however, the booming of European-made guns was heard in tribal feuds. In return for guns and other gifts, the Frenchmen acquired animal furs that brought high prices in Europe.

The French, disturbed by the natives' appearance and some of their customs, called them "savages." (Some of the Indians undoubtedly thought the Europeans who invaded their hunting grounds were no less savage.) Yet the French developed close friendships with some of the Indian tribes. From them, French hunters learned to wear snowshoes— flat, webbed devices worn with their boots that helped them walk faster over soft, snow-covered ground. They learned how to cut maple tree trunks at a certain time of year to draw syrup. They learned to propel bark canoes through river rapids. They learned to grow and cook new kinds of food, such as Indian corn and pumpkins.

The French found the Native Americans sometimes frightening, but also impressive, even beautiful. Giovanni da Verrazano described the men of one tribe as being larger than the Europeans. "[T]hey are of the color of brass, some of them incline more to whiteness: others are of yellow color . . . with long and black hair, which they are very careful to trim and deck up. . . . The women are of the like conformity and beauty: very handsome and well favored, of pleasant countenance, and comely to behold . . . well mannered . . . and of good education."

Jacques Cartier, writing of a different tribe, described the men as "untamed and savage. They wear their hair bound on top of their heads like a fistful of twisted hay, sticking into it a pin or something and adding birds' feathers. They are clothed in peltry [animal skins], men and women alike, but women shape theirs more to their figures and gird their waists. They paint themselves with tan colors. They have boats in which they go to sea made of birch bark."

For the most part, the Native Americans did much more for the French than the French did for them. In many ways, the foreigners brought misery with them. The French introduced the natives to firearms, valuable for hunting, but they also introduced them to alcohol, which sometimes made the Indians senseless and violent. The Europeans brought to America diseases that the Indians never had suffered from before. Whole native villages were killed by smallpox and other illnesses the Indians did not know how to treat.

Although the French explorers had come to North America hoping to find gold and spices, they soon found another source of riches—furs. Because furs were valuable in Europe, French trappers and traders could make a lot of money from the fur trade. At right is the pelt of a red fox, hanging in a trader's log cabin, while the hide of a deer is being stretched on a wooden frame in the lower photograph.

The thing that kept the Indians at peace with the French intruders was trade. While the French were taking away countless animal pelts, they also were bringing to the New World items the Indians wanted. A small hand mirror or a sewing needle may seem of little value to us today, but to Native Americans who had never before seen or used such items, they were in great demand. At the same time, the elk, lynx, and other furs that brought so much money in European society were common, everyday items in the

A Hard Life

Life for the first European settlers in America was extremely hard. It was especially difficult for white Catholic missionaries who came to teach, tend, and convert the Native Americans. The priests, whom the Indians called "Black Robes" (their long, black robes particularly impressed the natives), and nuns were at the forefront in establishing relations between the French and Indians—and they sometimes paid for their boldness with their lives.

Some missionaries fell to sickness in the cold wilderness, others to the spear and tomahawk of hostile Indians. If tribal medicine men or warriors convinced a group of natives that the missionaries were enemies, they often tortured the clerics to a slow death with fire, horrible surgical procedures, or brute force.

Indian villages.

The French traders and trappers sought one type of animal skin more than others. It was the fur of the beaver, used by European designers to make hats. The hats became very popular and so brought high prices. The rough French traders in the New World scrambled to find more beaver pelts. Some of them became quite wealthy.

Although the French and Indians generally lived in peace, violence did erupt, however—sometimes with catastrophic results. French settlers constantly had to guard against hostile natives.

In time, the French also were challenged by European settlers from other nations. Ultimately, the Europeans' struggle for control of the new continent would result in full-scale wars.

All the while, the French commanders worried about mutiny from within. Many of their settlers were bad-tempered criminals—outcasts from the home country. They frequently caused trouble in the settlements.

Among the more tragic victims of these fights were the Huguenots who tried to settle the lower coast of North America. Ironically, the Huguenots came to America in part to escape violence. In France and other European countries during the 1500s and 1600s, a heated and sometimes violent clash of religions was waged between Roman

Catholics and Protestants. Protestants were church scholars and citizens who opposed certain practices of the Roman Catholic Church.

Huguenots were French Protestants. During the 1550s, the Huguenots grew in number. They faced increasing *persecution* by certain French nobles allied with the Catholic Church. Soon, this tension erupted into civil war. Before it was over, thousands of people would be slaughtered and several royal and church leaders assassinated.

Admiral Gaspard de Coligny was a Huguenot leader. Hoping to find a solution to the persecution in France, he sent an expedition under the command of Jean Ribaut to establish a Huguenot colony in the New World. In 1562,

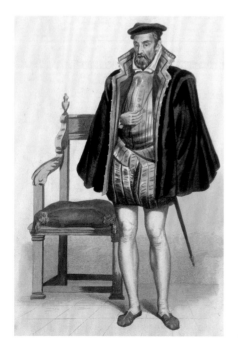

The French Huguenot leader Gaspard de Coligny inspired several attempts to establish French settlements along the southeastern coast of North America.

Ribaut's party arrived at the mouth of the Broad River in South Carolina and set about building a small settlement.

After Ribaut left them to return to France, the settlers behaved foolishly, failing to plant crops and gather food. The natives in the area were friendly, giving the French food and treating them like kings, but the wasteful Europeans soon abandoned their settlement and left the New World, sailing for the Netherlands.

Two years later, another French group built a fort on the St. John's River in northern Florida. They called it Fort Caroline, after King Charles. The great danger here was the presence of Spanish soldiers not far away. In the summer of 1565 a Spanish force destroyed the French village and slaughtered most of the French colonists.

In 1567, a French commander named Dominique de Gourges sailed from France with a small force to attack the Spaniards who had slain their comrades. They got their revenge. Aided by natives in the area, they killed many Spanish soldiers. The French effort to colonize the south-eastern coast, however, was over.

Even in peaceful times, life in the New World was hard and somewhat primitive for the Europeans, whether they were common farmers and fishermen or refined members of the upper class. They had to endure withering heat and clouds of mosquitoes in summer and freezing temperatures

The Early French Explorers of North America

A reconstruction of Fort Caroline, the French fort established by Protestant Huguenots in present-day Florida. The garrison at the fort was eventually killed by Spaniards from nearby St. Augustine.

in winter. Even indoors, it was so cold in Canada that some early settlers built enclosed, cabinet-like beds to sleep in. In the short-lived Florida colony, meanwhile, the weather posed a different threat: hurricanes. A Frenchman at Fort Caroline reported a storm "so great . . . that the Indians themselves assured me that it was the worst weather that ever was scene [sic] on that coast."

Furthermore, they lived in unhealthy conditions. The food sometimes was dirty, and for "napkins" to wipe their greasy fingers, the settlers used their clothes or the fur of dogs. (Indians reportedly wiped their hands in their hair.)

The settlers built outdoor ovens some distance from their dwellings to prevent cooking fires from spreading. Their wooden shelters would burn easily, and the threat of fire was one of the Europeans' worst fears.

Throughout the first century of French exploration and settlement in the New World, men and women came over the ocean with dreams of a better life. The life they found, however, was often harsh and relieved by few pleasures. With eyes constantly turned toward the Atlantic in springtime, exhausted survivors of the frigid winters hoped and waited for supply ships from their home country.

This statue of Samuel de Champlain over-
looks Chateau Frontenac, Quebec. In 1608
Champlain established a French settlement
at Quebec; it would soon become the most
important French outpost in the New
World. For his accomplishments, Champlain
has become known as the "father of
Canada."

The Founding of Quebec

IN 1603, ALMOST 80 years after Verrazano made the first official explorations of New France for King Francis I, a new adventurer arrived by ship at the entrance to the St. Lawrence River. Operating under the authority of France's King Henri IV, he would become the most famous of the early French leaders in New France. In fact, he is remembered today as the "father of Canada." His name was Samuel de Champlain.

Champlain was born in 1567 at Brouage, a French seaport. As a young man, he served in the French army, but soon directed his attention and energies toward the sea. From his first years as a sailor, he took careful notes, describing and mapping the places he visited. These observations were quite valuable to the early explorers in an era when most men of the sea could not read or write. Champlain earned a reputation as a man worth taking along on missions of importance.

By 1603, Champlain already was an experienced navigator who had traveled twice to the West Indies. Now, he was appointed pilot to an expedition led by François Gravé du Pont. He was told to make a detailed record of the mission for King Henri.

In late spring, the little fleet came to the French trading post of Tadoussac, not far inland from the broad mouth of the St. Lawrence. They traded with the Montagnais and Algonquin Indians, and Champlain led a small party to explore the area. He took excellent notes on the lay of the land and the smaller rivers that flowed into the St. Lawrence. The expedition then proceeded upriver to the Lachine Rapids before returning to France with the furs they had gathered.

Champlain returned to this area in 1604. This time, he was with a party that explored south of the Gulf of St. Lawrence, around present-day Nova Scotia and New Brunswick. They landed at an island they named St. Croix in Passamaquoddy Bay, at what is now the coastal boundary between New Brunswick and Maine. This was part of the

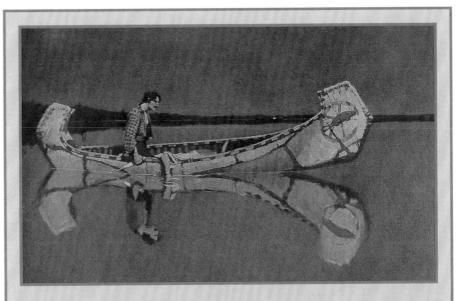

Traveling in New France

Birchbark canoes were to the northern Indians and early French-American traders what trucks are to society today. They carried many tons of animal hides from the North American wilderness over the Great Lakes and up the St. Lawrence and other rivers to French trading posts. They also carried European-made items—including guns and powder—into the wilderness, where they were traded to eager natives.

These large vessels, as the name suggests, were made from sections of birch tree bark. The Indians rubbed gum from spruce trees into the seams to make the canoe hulls waterproof. Both ends of the canoe were high and curled inward like the crest of a wave. Thus, they could be paddled in either direction. The high bow sections kept water from washing into the canoe in rough weather conditions.

Although the French king Henri IV gave his approval to Champlain's attempt to establish a permanent colony in North America, he did not provide very much money, supplies, or other support.

region the French explorers called Acadia. There, they built wooden huts to shelter them from the coming winter.

Not knowing what to expect from the severe winters of New France, Champlain and his men were not well prepared. The band of 80 adventurers was miserable on the cold, wind-blown island. Almost half of them died of scurvy. They realized—too late to relocate for the season—that there were no freshwater streams close by. They had to melt snow for their drinking water.

The next year, the survivors moved across the Bay of Fundy onto the mainland of Nova Scotia (which the French called Acadia). They had learned much, and they survived the next winter fairly secure, though not exactly comfortable. The following summer, 1606, more French settlers arrived with badly needed supplies. They planted crops and reaped a wonderful harvest. Champlain worked to keep up the colonists' spirits with games and jokes. It appeared the French settlement in Nova Scotia would last.

However, bad news soon came from France. Because of business and political rivalries, the French king had decided not to support the colony any longer. Knowing they could not survive cut off from the homeland, Champlain and the other colonists had to sail back to France.

Champlain had only begun his work in North America,

This painting shows a French settlement in Nova Scotia during the 18th century. Although Champlain had tried to plant a colony in the region as early as 1605, the earliest attempts to settle Acadia (as the French called the area) failed.

however. He wanted not only to explore the vast territory, but also to establish French towns in Acadia and along the St. Lawrence, and outposts far into the frontier.

In 1608, he brought a small band of hardy settlers to Stadacona. There, they established a settlement at "Kebec"—known today as Quebec. Champlain, now appointed deputy governor of New France, had noted the place during his 1603 visit and believed it would make a strong location for a fortress, easy to defend against attacks by Indians or marauding English.

Quebec became the capital of New France. Most of Canada, like the United States, gradually would forge its own identity—a blending of varied European and Native American influences—over the next four centuries. Interestingly, Quebec clings firmly to its French origins even today.

The early French in Quebec, however, barely survived. Of the 28 men Champlain brought with him to the settlement in 1608, only eight lived through the first winter. Again, scurvy—because of the settlers' limited diet—was the main cause of death. Champlain also was threatened with mutiny and had to have the leader of the plot executed. It was a tense beginning for what would become the first permanent white settlement in New France.

Under Champlain's leadership, New France became a

At Samuel de Champlain's order, French soldiers prepare to hang the leader of a plot to revolt against Champlain's leadership. Despite early problems, Quebec soon became one of the most important cities in New France.

gradually thriving, if seasonally bleak, European colony. He sent brave woodsmen to explore the territory in all directions and sometimes led expeditions himself. Soon after

While building his colony in New France, Champlain explored—or directed the exploration of—a large part of Canada and the northeastern United States.

establishing the Quebec colony, he took a band of men southward into what is now New York State.

Naturally, he was especially interested in what lay beyond the Lachine Rapids. Indians and French traders brought back exciting stories. One French woodsman, for example, told of finding the site of an English shipwreck in a great ocean to the west. Champlain went to see for himself. Though infuriated when he learned the story was false, he added to his store of knowledge of New France from this journey.

In 1615, he led a major expedition up the Ottawa River. They arrived at Georgian Bay on Lake Huron, then moved southeastward to Lake Ontario. During their yearlong adventure, Champlain made new friends among the natives—as well as enemies. In one battle against the

Onondaga tribe, Champlain took an arrow in the knee.

Champlain knew that in order for his own people to survive in New France and to prosper from trading or farming, they must get along with the natives. Champlain, therefore, established close ties to as many tribes as possible.

He apparently did not fully understand the problem this would cause. Different Indian peoples did not always get along with one another. That meant if the French made friends with one tribe, they became the enemies of that tribe's enemies. For example, Champlain forged **alliances** with the Hurons and Algonquins, and thus made an enemy of the Iroquois. The Iroquois made their own trading agreements with English colonists to the south. The French and English were bitter rivals. Iroquois hunting parties attacked French forts and outposts and kept the settlers living in fear.

Besides establishing French colonies, developing trade, and searching for the elusive shortcut to the Orient, Champlain had another objective in New France. He wished to convert the natives to Christianity. Champlain is believed to have been a Protestant by birth who eventually became a Catholic. The men who sailed with him were both Catholics and Protestants. (Religious tension was one of the ceaseless problems during Champlain's many years in New France.) By royal decree, the Indians in New France were to be converted to the Catholic faith.

The Protestants known as Huguenots tried to establish colonies on the southeastern coast of America. In New France to the north, meanwhile, the Catholic Church had taken the initiative to join explorers and colonists like Champlain. Catholic missionaries who came to convert the Indians needed the backing of the French government at home and in New France. The government, for its part, encouraged the missionaries. It would be much easier and less dangerous to deal with Christian Indians, Champlain knew, than with unfriendly savages who cared nothing for the Europeans or their way of life. The French government also left it to the missionaries to provide education for the natives and to operate frontier hospitals for French and Indians alike.

Quebec grew slowly. To most citizens of France, there was little attraction to that solitary outpost on the American frontier. Only a slow trickle of *emigrants* from France—adventurers, country *peasants* and city beggars with little to lose, Catholic missionaries, and prisoners from the country's crowded jails—arrived in Quebec during the next two centuries. They were sometimes hard to control. Indeed, Champlain's worst human threats came from within his city, not from the Indian nations outside. Yet these individuals helped build a city that would become world famous.

Elsewhere up and down the great St. Lawrence River, the followers of Champlain would leave their marks. To them, New France was a land where—if they could survive—farmers could clear land, plant crops, and claim it as their own. It was a land of hope for French families who dreamed of bettering their lives.

By the late 1620s, France was at war with its age-old enemy, England. From 1628–1629, an English naval force invaded the St. Lawrence, capturing the French ports of Tadoussac and Quebec. Champlain was arrested and sent to England, but eventually was released to France. By treaty, France got back its old territory in the New World.

Champlain returned to Quebec in 1633 to resume his work. He had more land cleared around the town, put up new buildings, and did what he could to improve relations with the Indians. He died on Christmas Day 1635 in Quebec.

As a founder of New France, Champlain must have felt in his heart that he was a failure. In the warmer climate to the south, he knew that France's English rivals were prospering in large settlements along the New England and Virginia coasts. Those colonists endured hardships of their own, but not the hardships of frostbite that required *amputation*, or rivers that froze over for two to three months each year, making travel impossible.

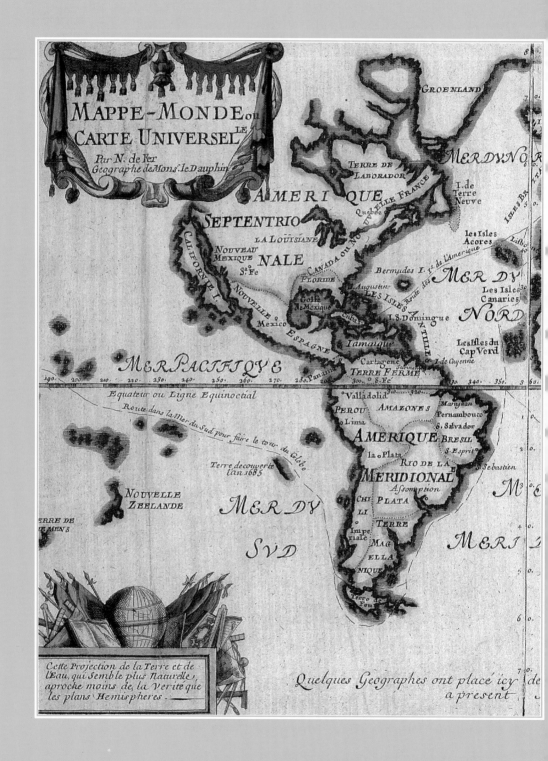

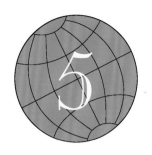

To the Great Lakes and Beyond

AFTER 1616, SAMUEL de Champlain was too busy governing and drumming up support for the French settlements and trading operations along the St. Lawrence River to lead further expeditions himself. Ambitious young Frenchmen took up the investigation instead, exploring hundreds of miles along the waterways and into the deep forests. Two of the most notable pioneers were Étienne Brûlé and Jean Nicolet.

Brûlé, a French peasant from the town of Champigny-sur-Marne near Paris, was in his early teens when he came to New France in 1608 as part of Champlain's Kebec colony. Young Brûlé took a serious interest in the Native

51

Americans. After he mastered the tongue of the Montagnais people, Champlain thought it would be useful to send him to live with the Algonquins for a while and learn the Indian ways. Brûlé soon became so fascinated by the ruggedly beautiful forests and rivers and their inhabitants that he decided to spend his life in the wilderness. He learned other Indian languages and became an important interpreter between the French and the Native Americans. He even dressed and lived as the Indians did.

While roaming the woods with his Indian friends, Brûlé saw many places never before visited by Europeans. Historians believe he may have been the first white person to explore the banks of Lake Huron. He also is thought to have traveled far to the south into what is today Pennsylvania and the upper Chesapeake Bay region.

A special type of person was now coming to prominence in New France: the *coureurs de bois*. The French term means "runners of the woods." Brûlé was one of them. These were sturdy, weatherworn Frenchmen who lived with the Indians or alone in the forests. They collected animal skins in the wild, then packed them into canoes and paddled them to the trading settlements. The life of a woods runner was toilsome and dangerous, with few comforts—but it could be remarkably profitable.

The law required that *coureurs de bois* obtain licenses

The Great Lakes—Lake Erie, Lake Huron, Lake Ontario, Lake Michigan, and Lake Superior—compose the largest connected area of fresh water on earth. In fact, Lake Superior is larger than any other freshwater lake in the world. When the French woodsmen of the 17th century arrived at the Great Lakes, the waterways served as an entrance to the interior of North America.

from the colonial governor in order to trade furs. Some young men, in their *zeal* for riches, ignored the law and became renegade traders.

Legal or not, these frontiersmen had dangerous, difficult careers. Some were drowned in river rapids trying to manage their fur-laden birchbark canoes. Some died of diseases such as smallpox, dysentery, malaria, and tuberculosis. Others ran afoul of the natives and were murdered, or were attacked by bears or wolf packs. More than one woodsman set out into the wilderness never to be heard from again.

Like many early American explorers, Étienne Brûlé came to a tragic end. During his years of living with the Indians, he occasionally had known their wrath as well as their kindness. (At one point, hostile natives had tortured him by biting out his fingernails.) He always had survived and continued his beloved free life in the wilds. But in 1833, he ran afoul of some of the Hurons. They brutally executed him, then ate his flesh!

By this time, other Frenchmen had reached the Great Lakes. Father Joseph le Caron was one of the missionaries Champlain had encouraged to live among the natives and convert them. Le Caron lived with the Huron Indians and ventured as far as Lake Huron—which he at first thought might be the sea leading to the Orient until he tasted the water and found it was not salty.

Another frontiersman took up the challenge of exploring. Jean Nicolet, born in Cherbourg, France in 1598, came to America as one of Champlain's colonists. He arrived in 1618 and, like Brûlé, lived for some time among the Indians and learned their languages and ways of life. According to an early historical account, while living with the natives, Nicolet sometimes "passed seven or eight days without eating anything; he was seven whole weeks without other nourishment than a little bark."

Nicolet, who became one of the official French interpreters in the New World, set out from Quebec in 1634. He hoped to find the waterway that would lead through North America and into the Pacific Ocean. Even at this late date—more than a century after Verrazano's voyages—the French were still looking for the mythical shortcut to the Orient. Nicolet, in fact, took with him a Chinese silk robe; he wanted to be dressed appropriately if he encountered the Orientals.

The ambitious wanderer obviously never got near China, but he did play an important role in expanding the French influence across Canada. Reaching Lake Michigan and the land of modern-day Wisconsin, he established trade agreements with local Indians. At this point, he was near the headwaters of the great Mississippi River.

Like so many before him, Nicolet was fooled by the

The work of French explorers like Cartier, Champlain, Brûlé, and Nicolet paved the way for later Frenchmen to explore even further into the interior of North America. During the late 17th century, such adventurers as Father Jacques Marquette, Louis Joliet, and René-Robert Cavelier, Sieur de La Salle would range far into the interior of North America. This painting shows LaSalle's ships landing on the Gulf of Mexico, where he hoped to start a French colony. Louisiana, and the city of New Orleans, would eventually become important French settlements in North America.

Great Lakes. When he heard of the Winnebago Indians, he interpreted their tribal name as "dwellers by the sea." Their "sea," he reasoned excitedly, must be the Pacific Ocean.

However, it proved to be only a lake. In the end, the land around Lake Michigan was as close to the Pacific as Nicolet ever ventured.

Popular among both the Indian natives and French settlers, Nicolet resumed his important role as interpreter in Quebec. He married a goddaughter of Champlain in 1637. In 1642, while traveling by canoe to try to negotiate the release of an Indian prisoner, Nicolet died when the vessel sank in a violent storm on the St. Lawrence.

A generation later, other French explorers, such as Marquette and La Salle, would travel down the Mississippi River and prove there was, in fact, no waterway through North America to the Pacific Ocean. This would disappoint European kings and merchants, who hoped to take advantage of a fast sea route to the riches of the Orient.

By that time, however, a small but determined population of French farmers, hunters, fishermen, traders, and missionaries would be firmly settled in New France. Following the examples of Cartier, Champlain, and other early explorers, they gave France its roots in North America.

Chronology

1524   King Francis I of France sends Giovanni da Verrazano, a navigator from Italy, to try to find a westward sea route to the Orient; Verrazano explores the eastern coast of New France, now modern-day Canada.

1528   Verrazano is apparently murdered by natives in the Caribbean Sea.

1534   Jacques Cartier's first expedition to North America arrives at Newfoundland in May. After he claims the Gaspé peninsula for France, he returns home in September.

1535   During his second visit to North America, Cartier explores the St. Lawrence River. He spends a miserable winter in the woods, and returns to France in 1536.

1541   Cartier returns to North America (now called New France).

1542   Jean-François de La Rocque, Sieur de Roberval, arrives in New France to establish a colony along the St. Lawrence River; Cartier leaves and returns home to France.

1543   Roberval and the survivors of his colony return to France.

1557   Jacques Cartier dies near St. Malo, France.

1562   Huguenots led by Jean Ribaut attempt to settle on the southeastern coast of North America, but eventually abandon their settlement.

Chronology

1564 Huguenots build Fort Caroline, but the fort is destroyed the next year by Spanish troops from St. Augustine.

1603 Samuel de Champlain accompanies a French expedition on his first of many voyages to the New World.

1608 Champlain founds Quebec; Étienne Brûlé arrives in New France as a teenager. Until his murder by Indians 25 years later, he will live and travel with the Indians, exploring as far west as Lake Huron and as far south as the upper Chesapeake Bay.

1618 Jean Nicolet arrives in New France. He will explore as far west as modern-day Wisconsin.

1629 An English naval raid captures Quebec. Champlain is arrested and sent to England.

1635 After returning to Quebec to continue his work, Champlain dies.

1642 Jean Nicolet drowns in the St. Lawrence River.

Glossary

alliance—a written or verbal agreement between people or nations by which they pledge to trade with one another or help one another in times of war.

amputation—the cutting off of an injured or diseased limb from the body in order to prevent infection from spreading.

colony—a place inhabited and controlled by citizens and officials of a foreign country.

commission—the granting of a military or government title and authority to an individual.

corsair—a pirate.

emigrant—a person who leaves his or her native country to go live in another place.

expedition—a journey by a group of people with a specific trading or exploration goal.

mariner—a fisher, trader, or explorer who travels the open sea.

mutiny—a revolt by a ship crew or army unit against the commander.

navigator—one who sets and follows a course across sea or land, using a compass and other instruments combined with astronomical markers (such as the North Star and the sun) and known landmarks or features of the ocean.

Glossary

peasant—a member of a lower, often uneducated, social class who works the land for others.

persecution—ridicule or cruel treatment of one person or group by another.

pow wow—a Native American ceremony featuring dancing, feasting, and singing in which many tribes often took part.

rendezvous—a meeting place.

scurvy—a painful disease caused by lack of vitamin C, with symptoms such as swelling flesh and rotting gums.

transatlantic—across the Atlantic Ocean.

trinket—a small article of little value, such as an ornament or piece of inexpensive jewelry.

viceroy—governor of a colony.

zeal—energetic enthusiasm or excitement about something.

Further Reading

Coulter, Tony. *Jacques Cartier, Samuel de Champlain, and the Explorers of Canada*. Philadelphia: Chelsea House Publishers, 1993.

Faber, Harold. *The Discoverers of America*. New York: Charles Scribner's Sons, 1992.

Harmon, Daniel E. *Jacques Cartier and the Exploration of Canada*. Philadelphia: Chelsea House Publishers, 2001.

Riendeau, Roger. *A Brief History of Canada*. New York: Facts on File, Inc., 2000.

Wartik, Nancy. *The French Canadians*. New York/Philadelphia: Chelsea House Publishers, 1989.

Internet Resources

Information about the early French explorers

http://geonames.nrcan.gc.ca/education/index_e.php

http://www.enchantedlearning.com/explorers/page/l/lasalle.shtml

http://www2.worldbook.com/wc/popup?path=features/explorers&page=html/saga_na_after.html&direct=yes

http://www.mce.k12tn.net/explorers/frenchexplorers.htm

http://www.heritage.nf.ca/exploration/engfrench.html

http://www.geo.msu.edu/geo333/french_explorers.html

Index

Photo Credits

About the Author

Daniel E. Harmon of Spartanburg, South Carolina, has written 30 books and numerous articles on topics ranging from history to humor. He is the editor of *The Lawyer's PC*, a national computer newsletter, and associate editor of *Sandlapper: The Magazine of South Carolina.*